MONSTERS

GENIES

BY BONNIE JUETTNER

KIDHAVEN PRESS
A part of Gale, Cengage Learning

GALE
CENGAGE Learning™

Detroit • New York • San Francisco • New Haven, Conn • Waterville, Maine • London

Every effort has been made to trace the owners of copyrighted material.

LIBRARY OF CONGRESS CATALOGING-IN-PUBLICATION DATA

Juettner, Bonnie.
  Genies / by Bonnie Juettner.
     p. cm. -- (Monsters)
  Includes bibliographical references and index.
  ISBN 978-0-7377-5051-5 (hardcover)
  1. Jinn--Juvenile literature. I. Title.
  GR549.J84 2010
  398'.4--dc22

                                                                2009045633

KidHaven Press
27500 Drake Rd.
Farmington Hills, MI 48331

ISBN-13: 978-0-7377-5051-5
ISBN-10: 0-7377-5051-0

Printed in the United States of America
1 2 3 4 5 6 7 14 13 12 11 10

Printed by Bang Printing, Brainerd, MN, 1st Ptg., 06/2010

CONTENTS

CHAPTER 1

FIERY DESERT SPIRITS

Travelers to the deserts of North Africa and the Middle East must be careful. Dying a slow death from dehydration (a lack of water) and sun exposure is not the worst thing that can happen to a wayfarer in the desert. In fact, death by dehydration might be kind, compared to what could happen. The worst fate might be to meet a **genie.** Genies are fiery desert spirits who can change shape. They have supernatural powers, and sometimes they are pure evil. Fiery desert spirits are not always called genies—sometimes they are called jinn or djinn.

4

ALADDIN'S LAMP

Deserts in the United States are not known for attracting genies. Most Americans know little about genies aside from the story of Aladdin—a Middle Eastern story that comes from the book *1001 Arabian Nights*. In the story, a teenage Aladdin is tricked by a magician who pretends to be his uncle. The magician opens a hole in the ground that leads to an underground palace, and he sends Aladdin into the palace to retrieve a lamp. But Aladdin and the magician argue because Aladdin refuses to turn over the lamp until he has climbed out of the hole. Angry, the magician closes the opening in the ground, sealing Aladdin in total darkness in the underground palace with the lamp.

Aladdin spends three days underground, expecting to die. He has no food or water. But the magician had given him a ring to keep him safe while he was underground. On the third day, Aladdin accidentally rubs the ring, and a horrendous, terribly ugly being appears. It is a genie, so tall that its head touches the roof of the palace. The people who first told this story imagined this genie with knotted hair and giant teeth, because that is what most genies in Arabian folktales looked like.

The genie asks Aladdin, "What dost thou command?" Aladdin asks to be rescued from the underground palace. The genie grants his wish, and Aladdin goes home to his mother and tells her ev-

People who first told the story of Aladdin's Lamp probably imagined a genie with knotted hair and giant teeth.

erything. To prove that he is telling the truth, he hands her the lamp and shows her the magician's ring. As she listens, Aladdin's mother begins to clean the lamp and another genie appears. The genie asks, "What are thy commands?"[1] Aladdin's mother faints in fear and horror, but Aladdin asks for food. When his mother recovers, she tells Aladdin that he should get rid of the ring and the lamp, because it is too dangerous to get involved with genies. But Aladdin keeps both, and uses the services of the two genies to make himself wealthy. Eventually,

after many adventures, he has become so wealthy that he manages to marry a princess.

THE FISHERMAN AND THE GENIE

Most of the genies in Middle Eastern folktales are much more frightening than the genie in the Aladdin story. In one story, a fisherman opens a bottle that he finds in the ocean, and smoke floats out of the bottle. When the smoke clears, a genie is standing there. The genie is so huge that its head touches the clouds, while its feet remain on the ground. The genie says, "Ask of me only what mode of death thou wilt die, and by what manner of slaughter I shall slay thee."[2] The fisherman protests that he should be rewarded, not punished, for letting the genie out of the bottle. But the genie explains that he has been in the bottle a very long time. After the first 100 years, the genie promised himself that he would make whoever released him a wealthy man for the rest of his life. After 400 years, he decided that whoever released him would receive three wishes. Finally he decided that he would kill whoever released him and that person could choose how to die.

Fortunately the fisherman manages to trick the genie back into the bottle. He asks the genie to prove that it is really possible for such a giant genie to fit in such a tiny bottle. The fisherman then puts the stopper back in the bottle and throws the bottle back into the sea.

ANCIENT LEGENDS

Both the story of Aladdin and the story of the fisherman and the genie came from the same book, *1001 Arabian Nights*. The original versions of all

A painting of a genie appearing from a lamp. This page came from the story of the fisherman and the genie found in the book 1001 Arabian Nights.

the stories in *1001 Arabian Nights* were ancient Persian and Arabian folktales, believed to date from the 900s. The time period when the *1001 Arabian Nights* stories were written is now called the golden age of Islam. During the golden age of Islam, art, literature, science, math, philosophy, and technology all flourished. It lasted from about the 800s to the 1400s.

Although the stories in *1001 Arabian Nights* were written down during the golden age of Islam, they are probably much older. They come from ancient Middle Eastern folklore. Unlike many other monster stories, stories about genies do not come from all over the world. Genie stories come mainly from the Middle East and Africa. Some genie stories come from places near the Middle East, such as India. Some stories come from Eastern European countries, such as Serbia and Albania. Genie stories probably arose in the Middle East because the Middle East is the birthplace of Judaism, Christianity, and Islam. The genies that became a part of Islamic folklore are very much like the demons that many Christian and Jewish stories describe.

DESERT SPIRITS

No matter where they came from, genies were said to have an unusual ability–they could change form. Their natural form was **vapor**, a kind of mist or smoke. This is how genies got into and out of bottles and lamps in which they were sometimes trapped. Trapping a genie in a container was one of the few ways a human could control a genie.

Because they were not solid, genies could also **shape-shift**, changing themselves into human or animal form. For example, legends of the Songhai, a people of West Africa, say that evil genies liked to take the form of cats and dogs, especially black cats and dogs. They would shape-shift into these animals in order to prowl through the villages at night. In animal form, however, genies were thought to be vulnerable. They had to obey the rules of whatever form they took. If a human killed a cat or dog that was really a genie, then the genie died too.

According to Middle Eastern legends, genies could also **possess** a human body. They could take control of it and make it say and act in ways that the genie chose. Genies sometimes possessed a human and forced him or her to yawn uncontrollably, for their own amusement. But forced yawning was the kindest of the tricks that a genie would play while possessing a human. Sometimes they drove the humans they possessed insane or took possession of their bodies permanently. In ancient times, people who talked in gibberish were thought to be communicating with genies who were possessing them.

It was thought that genies rarely interacted with humans, though, and when they did, it usually happened by accident. Occasionally a genie, for one reason or another, deliberately chose to contact a human. Sometimes humans managed to trap and

Genies

control genies, by binding them magically to an object, such as a lamp, a ring, or a bottle. But only magicians could do this by casting a magic spell.

GODLIKE POWERS

The ancient Semites lived in the Middle East prior to the development of Judaism. (Their **descendants** later became Jews and Arabs.) Semites thought that genies were the spirits of vanished ancient peoples. But unlike ghosts, genies had special powers that were similar to the powers of gods. In ancient times, people did not understand how diseases spread, or what mental illness was, or how weather patterns formed. Instead the Semites thought genies could cause disease and that genies were responsible for

The ancient Arabs believed that genies were fiery spirits that had godlike abilities. It was thought that these genies could create wealth for the person who freed them from a bottle or lamp.

making some people become mentally ill. They also thought that genies could change the weather. They believed that genies could charm horses so that a storm would follow the horse wherever it went when the horse was ridden.

The ancient Arabs had similar ideas about genies. But they did not view genies as ghosts. Instead they considered genies to be fiery spirits that lived in the desert. Like the Semites, Arabs believed that these spirits had special powers. The genies of some of their stories have godlike abilities. They can create something out of nothing. They can grant wishes. These genies could perhaps be described as **demigods**, beings who have some, but not all, of the powers of a god. The genies in *1001 Arabian Nights* have this kind of power. They can create wealth for the person who frees them from a bottle or lamp, but they also have the power to destroy their rescuers.

In Arabic folklore, some genie stories are considered fiction, while other stories are believed to be absolutely true. Genies appear in ancient Arab zoological encyclopedias and in Arab legal handbooks. Genies also can be found in ancient Arab legal documents, where their standing is discussed with regard to questions of marriage, death, property ownership, and inheritance. Not only ancient peoples believed in genies. People in many twenty-first-century cultures also consider genies to be utterly real.

CHAPTER 2

TRAVELERS BEWARE!

According to Persian mythology, many travelers have been tricked by **ghouls**, one of the most dangerous and mean types of genie. Ghouls are said to have faces covered by shaggy, tangled hair that hangs over their eyes and hooves for feet. They also have sharp claws and teeth, and their jaws are stained with blood. Ghouls particularly like to live in places where humans have died, such as battlefields and murder sites. They like deserts, where many people have died of thirst and exposure. They also like cemeteries. Ghouls sometimes rob graves and eat the dead, so they are sometimes confused with zombies. But ghouls are

13

A person dressed as a goul. Ghouls are considered the most dangerous and malicious of all genies species and according to Persian mythology have tricked many desert travelers.

not zombies. They are evil genies.

At night in the desert, ghouls light fires and sing songs to convince travelers that they are human. A ghoul may even shape-shift into the form of a beautiful woman. A traveler who gets close will be able to see that even in the shape of a beautiful woman, a ghoul still has hoofed feet. A traveler who thinks that he or she has just met a shape-shifting ghoul can ask it whether it is a ghoul. It is believed that ghouls, and other genies, have to tell the truth. A traveler can also light a candle to identify a ghoul. The act of lighting a candle forces a ghoul to return to its natural shape. But by the time a traveler gets close enough to see the ghoul's feet, ask it a question, or light a candle, it may be too late. Once a ghoul has cornered a traveler alone, it will show its claws, rip apart its prey, and devour it whole. Some ghouls, however, may keep their prey alive in order to terrorize or possess it.

Some storytellers consider the **succubus** to be a kind of ghoul. A succubus always takes the form of a beautiful woman. But a woman who is really a succubus may also have nonhuman traits, such as batlike wings, horns, a tail with a spaded tip, snakelike eyes, and, like other ghouls, hoofed feet. The succubus particularly targets male travelers. It has the ability to appear to men in their dreams, giving them dreams that they cannot forget even when awake. Rather than ripping a man apart and eating his flesh, as other ghouls do, a succubus will slowly drain a man's energy until he is dead.

ESCAPE

Luckily it is possible to escape from a ghoul. The only way to do so at close range is to show the ghoul kindness. A quick-thinking traveler may offer to cut and comb the ghoul's tangled facial hair so that the ghoul can see well. It is believed that a ghoul will go out of its way to help a traveler who shows this sort of kindness. In Hebrew and Arabic, a female ghoul is called a **sila**. Both male and female ghouls like to kidnap human children. If a human baby or toddler nurses at the breast of a sila, she will treat him or her as well as she does her own children, taking care of the baby or toddler with great kindness.

Travelers can also escape from a ghoul if they recognize the creature as a ghoul while still at a distance. One story tells of a messenger who was sent along a road that passes through the Valley of the Angel of Death, a valley between the cities of Tehran and Kum in the country of Iran. This valley is said to be a particular favorite of ghouls. While camping at night, the messenger saw two ghouls on the horizon. He was not sure that they were ghouls until daybreak, when he saw them evaporate. (In some traditions, it is thought that ghouls come out only at night.) On seeing this, the messenger realized that he had just seen two ghouls and turned back, certain that he should not pass that way.

There is a third way to escape from a ghoul. It is

possible to kill a ghoul. But the ghoul must be killed swiftly, with one blow. A second blow, it is said, will bring the ghoul back to life.

AFRITS

A ghoul is one of two types of genies that are regarded throughout the Arab world as horrifying. The other kind is an **afrit**. Afrits live in deserted places, such as desert wastelands. Afrits are extremely powerful genies. They are big and very tall. Like ghouls they have hoofed feet, but afrits also have horns on their heads. They are so mean to humans that it is said that merely mentioning an afrit to an Arab causes him or her to feel unspeakable terror.

Afrits are extremely powerful types of genies. They often strike terror into people because of their gigantic appearance, hoofed feet, and horns on their heads.

The mention of ghouls and afrits causes terror because one never knows when a ghoul or an afrit may be around. All genies have the ability to be invisible. In fact, it is said that genies are invisible most of the time, unless they choose to show themselves. Some genies are as numerous in the desert as grains of sand, but that humans simply cannot see them most of the time. Ancient Jewish books say that every human has thousands of genies at his or her side at all times. The air is full of them. So the idea of mentioning the name of a terrifying kind of genie is frightening itself, because it might inspire the genie to show itself.

Even when genies were not mentioned by name, invisible genies floating through the air were considered terrifying. People long ago believed that humans could accidentally swallow a genie, making them sick. Diseases, in ancient times, were called fiends, or evil supernatural beings. A sick person might be said to be afflicted by the cholera fiend, or the influenza fiend. The Arabic word for madness, or mental illness, is *majnoon*, which literally means "possessed by jinni." The only way to cure a sick person was to force the genie to leave the body with prayers or recitations of scripture.

An Underground World

Not all genies, however, cared to possess or terrify humans. According to Persian mythology, not all genies were evil. Some were good, while others did

not care about humans at all. These genies lived in an underground genie community called **Jinnistan**. The underground genie world was much like the human world. But there were some important differences. Genies had communities, like human communities. Genies ate food, as humans do, but genie food was made of bones and animal dung. Genies married each other and had children. They had their own jobs, such as making jewelry. It was said that no human could copy the intricate designs made by genie jewelers living in Jinnistan. Like humans, eventually genies died, although they lived a lot longer than humans did. Compared to humans, genies seemed immortal, because they could live for thousands of years.

Not all genies lived in Jinnistan. In Middle Eastern mythology, genies are said to have lived in many remote places, such as underground caves. Evil genies, such as ghouls, were frequently found in the desert, but so were good genies. When not there, they could be found near or in caves, wells, and **cisterns**.

Some cultures believed that caves and wells might be entrances to Jinnistan, which lay deep underground, in the seventh layer of the Earth. But in Kenya, a country in East Africa, genies who lived in rivers and pools were said to do so for evil reasons. If a child wandered near a deep pool without supervision, a genie would appear, grab the child by the legs, and pull it underwater, holding it there

until it drowned.

In ancient times, genies were thought to be capable of great harm. In some African cultures, people who were badly injured, paralyzed, or insane, were thought to be suffering from the wrath of a genie. At the same time, people who were very wealthy or successful were thought to have befriended a genie with some act of thoughtfulness or kindness.

Genies

Middle Eastern mythology states that genies can live in many remote places, including cisterns like this one.

Genies liked to tease and trick people. An invisible genie might push a person down a flight of stairs, just for fun. But most genies did not cause harm unless they were angry or annoyed or if a human ignored a genie's rules. Some genies, living in later times, were thought to be good-hearted enough that they could convert to human religions.

CHAPTER 3

ARE GENIES REAL?

Most people living in the United States and western Europe consider genies to be fantastic, mythical creatures. However, not all people around the world agree. Many people believe in genies. Genies are an important part of many African cultures and religions, especially in North Africa. Genies are also frequently mentioned in the Qur'an (also spelled Koran), the sacred book of Islam. Experts of Islam say that genies are real. They consider the demons mentioned by Christian, Hindu, and Buddhist scriptures to be genies with different names.

IBLIS

Jewish, Christian, and Islamic scriptures all contain a similar creation story. God creates a human male (Adam) and a human female (Eve) out of clay and places them in the Garden of Eden to live. He warns Adam and Eve that they can eat any fruit in the garden except for the fruit of the tree of knowledge of good and evil. But a snake comes and tempts Eve, suggesting that she try the forbidden fruit. Eve does, and then she offers some to Adam. In the Christian Bible, the snake is really the devil, or Satan—a fallen angel. In Islam, however, the snake is understood to be a genie. According to Middle Eastern mythology, genies love to shape-shift into snake form. The snake who tempted Eve is believed to be an evil genie named **Iblis**. He is sometimes called **Azazel**, the prince of darkness, or al-Shairan, the "enemy of God." Religion experts also believe that the demons who tempted Jesus in the desert in the New Testament were actually genies.

In the Qu'ran's version of the story of the Garden of Eden, Iblis goes to Eve in snake form and whispers to her. He tells her that unless she eats of the fruit of the tree of knowledge, she will never be able to have children. As a result of this, Eve decides to try the fruit.

In the Judeo-Christian tradition, Satan is thought to have been an angel who rebelled against God and fell from grace, becoming evil. Muslims (people who practice Islam), however, do not believe that Satan was ever an angel. The Qu'ran describes three classes of beings that were created by Allah, or God. Allah is said to have created the angels out of light, humans out of clay, and genies—a class between angels and humans—out of smokeless fire. Smokeless fire is different from ordinary fire in that it does not burn. This kind of fire is called **subtle fire**. In the Islamic version of the creation story, Allah orders both the angels and the genies to bow down before humanity. The angels and many of the genies obey, but Iblis refuses. As a being made of fire, Iblis was said to have considered himself superior to a being such as a human, who was made merely of earth. The stories say that Iblis became the leader of resistance against God's orders, or the being

Eve with the snake who tempted her to eat fruit from the tree of knowledge. According to Islam this snake is thought to be an evil genie named Iblis.

that Christians refer to as Satan. He vowed to tempt humans into disobeying God as well.

LILITH

Another story about the beginnings of humanity and genies is an ancient Jewish story that seems to fill in some gaps in the book of Genesis story in the Old Testament. In Genesis, God creates human beings twice. According to the story, "God created man in the image of himself, in the image of God he created them, male and female he created them."[3] But in the second chapter of Genesis, God creates a man from dust and creates a woman from the man's rib.

According to ancient Jewish legend, the woman who was created in Genesis was not Eve. It was Lilith. Lilith, however, much like Iblis, refused to obey Adam and left him. Then God created Eve so Adam would not be alone. Lilith, meanwhile, had children with Iblis. In the Jewish tradition, the children of Lilith and Iblis were demons. But experts of Islam view the children of Lilith and Iblis as genies. It is also believed that genies frequently hoped to have children with humans. Genies and humans, though, could not legally marry under Islamic law.

The story of Lilith and Iblis is not the only story of how genies come into existence. Some sources say that a person who dies in a state of great sin may be turned into a genie temporarily. In some Islamic countries, it is believed that Allah created

Adam's first wife Lilith kissing the snake Iblis. According to Islamic scholars the children of Lilith and Iblis are genies.

genies not out of fire, but out of a Sahara desert wind.

KING SOLOMON'S GENIES

According to Islamic legends, King Solomon had an army of genies. He controlled them with a magic ring. Some stories say that genies built Solomon's palace for him. Other stories say that Solomon called up his genies to help his armies when they went to a battle. The legends say that some genies

According to Muslim legends, King Solomon was thought to have an army of genies that he controlled with a magic ring.

refused to obey Solomon. These genies were sealed in jars and cast into the sea or forced to heat underground water forever, making hot springs.

Sakhr was one of the genies who rebelled against Solomon. He shape-shifted into the form of Solomon himself. Then he waited until Solomon took off his ring to take a bath. While Solomon was bathing, Sakhr snuck into the palace and asked Solomon's wife to give him Solomon's ring (pretending that it was his own ring, since he was in Solomon's shape). It is said that Sakhr ruled in Solomon's place for 40 days. But then Solomon managed to regain his throne, and he had Sakhr cast into Lake Tiberias with a stone around his neck.

Although many genies were evil, some genies were good, according to Islamic tradition. In fact, good genies can become members of a religious faith. One of the grandsons of Iblis, for example, is said to have become a Muslim during the time of King Solomon.

CHAPTER 4

GENIES WITH A SENSE OF HUMOR

One of the first modern stories about genies came from author Rudyard Kipling. Kipling lived in India during the late 1800s and based some of his stories on folktales that he heard there. Kipling's story "How the Camel Got His Hump" was published in 1902. In the story, the camel, unlike the other animals, refuses to do any work in the newly created world. Instead, he just says "Humph!"

Kipling writes that the Djinn of All Deserts goes to the camel and tells the camel to work. He warns the camel not to say "Humph!" again, but the camel does anyway. So the camel's back grows up into a

Rudyard Kipling wrote one of the first modern stories about genies. Kipling says that it was the Djinn of All Deserts that gave the camel his hump as punishment for not working in the newly created world.

"humph," or hump, that will allow him to work for three days without stopping to eat, because he had done no work for the first three days of the world. "Don't you ever say I never did anything for you," laughs the Djinn. "Humph yourself!"[4]

Genies as Comic Characters

Kipling was the first of a long line of modern authors to write about genies in a way that suggests that they are pranksters. One of the first authors to use humor in writing about a genie was Elizabeth Scarborough. In her 1984 novel, *The Harem of Aman*

Akbar, a princess who is kidnapped by a genie says that the genie did not want to kidnap her. The genie, she says, did not like her looks.

"He . . . deemed my substantial nose hideous," the princess confides to the novel's reader. "But this is typical of the djinn, who has lived a sheltered existence, for the most part, confined in his bottle." When the genie, who warns her that he is an afrit, arrives to kidnap her, the princess calls him a pipsqueak and refuses to go with him. She waves her knife at him and tells him, "Begone! Or I'll let the air out of you."[5] The genie makes her knife disappear, but the princess is not worried and demands that he leave ten horses for her family before he takes her anywhere. The genie agrees and he and the princess depart on a flying carpet.

THE CASTLE IN THE AIR

Six years later, Diana Wynne Jones followed in Scarborough's footsteps, writing about a genie who starts out scary and later becomes comical. Jones's genie in the book *The Castle in the Air* frightens the book's hero, Abdullah, at first by appearing suddenly and kidnapping the woman he loves. Jones writes:

> The cloud came right down into the lamplight. And it was not a cloud but great black leathery wings, silently beating. A pair of equally leathery arms, with hands that had

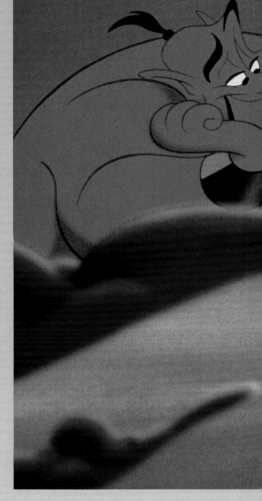

long fingernails like claws, reached from the shadow of those fanning wings and wrapped themselves around Flower-in-the-Night. . . . She looked around and up. Whatever she saw made her scream, one single wild, frantic scream, which was cut off when one of the leathery arms changed position to clap its huge taloned hand over her face. . . . For the merest instant Abdullah found himself staring into a hideous leathery face with a ring through its hooked nose and long, upslanting eyes, remote and cruel.[6]

It turns out that the genie is really a good genie who has been enslaved by a bad genie, his evil

brother. Still, this does not stop the genie from turning Abdullah into a toad, temporarily. "That'll teach you to pester me for extra wishes!"[7] he taunts Abdullah.

In 1992 Disney made a cartoon version of the Aladdin story. Disney hired actor Robin Williams to be the voice of the genie. Disney's movie made the genie character more fun than frightening. "Do you smoke?" he asks Aladdin when he first appears. When Aladdin shakes his head no, the genie retorts, "Mind if I do?"[8] and disappears into a puff of smoke.

A Genie Explosion

In recent years interest in genies has exploded. At least seven different new book series involving genies were published in the first decade of the twenty-first century. Authors Miranda Jones and Cindy Trumbore both published books for younger children that had genies as main characters. Jones's Little Genie series is about a genie who is a little girl. She is discovered by a human girl her own age, whose grandmother buys Little Genie's lamp for her at a garage sale. Trumbore's book, *The Genie in the Book*, is about a boy who accidentally releases a genie as he leafs through his mother's old copy of *1001 Arabian Nights*.

Author P.B. Kerr writes about child genies too. He created twin genies, the children of a genie mother and a human father, and describes them in his Children of the Lamp series. In the first book of the series, *The Akhenaten Adventure*, the twins discover that they are genies when they have their wisdom teeth removed at the age of twelve. The twins quickly begin to have strange symptoms. They feel cold in hot weather (genies like to be very warm). They begin to grow unusually fast, and the twin who had a problem with acne suddenly does not have acne anymore. And they accidentally grant wishes.

Then they go to visit their uncle Nimrod, who gives them each a copy of *1001 Arabian Nights* and happily informs them that they are both genies.

Jonathan Stroud, the author of the Bartimaeus Trilogy, takes a different approach. He writes about a world in which magicians get their power by harnessing demons and genies. Stroud's books are written from the point of view of a boy magician, who is terrified of genies but determined to master them, and from the point of view of the powerful genie that the boy manages to conjure out of thin air. While the boy, Nathaniel, takes himself very seriously, the genie, Bartimaeus, constantly makes sarcastic comments and jokes at his own expense, referring to himself as the "scourge of civilizations and the confidante of kings."[9] When Bartimaeus is near death from overwork, he still finds time for a sarcastic monologue about his plight. He says,

> Once, I was second to none. I could whirl through the air on a wisp of cloud and churn up dust storms with my passing. I could slice through mountains, raise castles on pillars of glass, fell forests with a single breath. I carved temples from the sinews of the earth and led armies against the legions of the dead, so that the harpers of a dozen lands played music in my memory and the chroniclers of a dozen centuries scribbled down my exploits. Yes! I was Bartimaeus—

Jonathan Stroud, author of the Bartimaeus Trilogy, a series of books about genies.

cheetah quick, strong as a bull elephant, deadly as a striking krait [poisonous snake]![10]

Now, explains Bartimaeus, he has become so weak that a public portapotty that fell over on him has trapped him on the sidewalk. "I was glad that no harpers or chroniclers [storytellers who recorded interesting events in ballads or stories so that future generations could remember them] happened to be passing,"[11] Bartimaeus confides.

To many people around the world, of course, genies are very real and still quite frightening. But modern fantasy writers are determined to show how human—and how prone to human mistakes and character flaws—genies can really be.

NOTES

CHAPTER 1: FIERY DESERT SPIRITS

1. Burton, Sir Richard, translator. "Aladdin; or, the Wonderful Lamp." *1001 Arabian Nights*. 1850 (translation date). http://www.sacred-texts.com/neu/burt1k1/tale30.htm.
2. Burton, Sir Richard, translator. "Aladdin; or, the Wonderful Lamp." *1001 Arabian Nights*. 1850 (translation date). http://www.sacred-texts.com/neu/burt1k1/tale30.htm.

CHAPTER 3: ARE GENIES REAL?

3. Genesis 1:27 (*The Jerusalem Bible*).

CHAPTER 4: GENIES WITH A SENSE OF HUMOR

4. Rudyard Kipling, *Just So Stories*, Puffin Classics, 2008, p. 18.
5. Elizabeth Scarborough, *The Harem of Aman Akbar*, New York: Bantam, 1984, p. 3.
6. Diana Wynne Jones, *Castle in the Air*, New York: Greenwillow, 1990, p. 40.
7. Jones, *Castle in the Air*, p. 58.
8. *Aladdin*, animated film, directed by Ron Clements and John Musker, Burbank, CA: Walt Disney Feature Animation, 1992. Transcript available at Internet Movie Script Database,www.imsdb.com/scripts/Aladdin.html.
9. Jonathan Stroud, *Ptolemy's Gate*, New York: Miramax, 2006, p. 11.
10. Stroud, *Ptolemy's Gate*, p. 11.
11. Stroud, *Ptolemy's Gate*, p. 12.

GLOSSARY

afrit: An extremely powerful genie that is as big as a giant.

Azazel: Another name for Iblis.

cisterns: Underground tanks where liquids, such as rainwater, are collected and stored.

demigods: Beings who have some, but not all, of the powers of a god.

descendants: People who come from a certain parent, usually someone earlier in the family line than a grandparent.

genie: Also called a jinni or djinni, a mythological spirit being that can appear as a monster, has supernatural abilities, and can live for thousands of years.

ghoul: A mean, dangerous genie that likes to lure innocent travelers to remote places and attack them.

Iblis: A genie that Muslims consider to be the devil.

Jinnistan: A mythical underground genie community.

possess: To enter into a living body and control its speech and actions.

shape-shift: To change into human or animal form, or appear as a vapor.

sila: A female ghoul.

subtle fire: The smokeless fire that genies are made of.

succubus: A kind of ghoul that always appears as a beautiful woman and that slowly drains the life energy out of its prey.

vapor: A kind of mist or smoke.

FOR FURTHER EXPLORATION

BOOKS

Judy Allen, Richard Hook, Jonathan Stroud, and John Howe, *Fantasy Encyclopedia*. London, England: Kingfisher, 2005. This is an encyclopedia of fantastic creatures, including many from the Middle East.

D.J. Conway, *The Ancient Art of Faery Magick*. Berkeley, CA: Crossing Press, 2005. This book treats genies as a species of fairy and includes many facts about genies, such as how to tell if you are talking to one.

Dinah Mack, *A Field Guide to Demons, Fairies, Fallen Angels, and Other Subversive Spirits*. New York: Little, Brown, 1998. This book is a good source for unusual facts about genies, with entries for different species of genie, such as ghouls, and for particular genies, such as Azazel.

Carol Rose, *Giants, Monsters, and Dragons: An Encyclopedia of Folklore, Legend, and Myth*. London: ABC-Clio, 2000. This is an encyclopedia of myths and folklore, including many entries on genies. It also offers information on ghouls and afrits.

J. Suter, *World Myths and Legends: Ancient Middle East.* Upper Saddle River, New Jersey: Globe Fearon, 1992. This book includes many ancient stories of genies and desert spirits and their interactions with humans.

WEB SITES

Encyclopedia Mythica (www.pantheon.org). This Web site is an online encyclopedia devoted to mythology. It includes entries on specific genies, such as Iblis and several of the sons of Iblis.

Internet Sacred Text Archive (www.sacred-texts.com/neu/burt1k1/index.htm). This Web site offers free online books about religion, folklore, and mythology, including the 1850 version of 1001 Arabian Nights.

INDEX

PICTURE CREDITS

ABOUT THE AUTHOR

Bonnie Juettner is a writer and editor of children's books and educational videos. She is also the mother of two children, both of whom are fascinated by genies. Juettner has a keen interest in mythology, science fiction, and fantasy. Her other books for Kidhaven Press's Monsters series include *Phoenix* and *Griffins*.